The Safety Book
Strangers and Dangers

by Yael Feder

Illustrations: Asya Aizenstein

Translated from the Hebrew: Jessica Setbon

Schocken Children's Books

I picked up Guy and Tammy from kindergarten today. Tammy gave me a BIG hug! Squeeze! Guy ran over to me. Zoom!
"Can we walk home today, Mommy?"
"Sure," I said with a smile. "There are always new and exciting things to discover on a walk."

We said goodbye as the teacher, Ms. Violet, patted the children's heads.

Guy, Tammy and I walked along together, two small hands in two big hands, a mom with her kids. We passed the corner store. Then we passed the big basketball court and stopped to watch some older children shooting hoops, just when we saw someone familiar in the distance.

"Look, there's Rachel's mommy," Tammy said.
She ran over to her and gave her a hug.

"My sister's a real hugger. She hugs everyone,"
Guy giggled, after Rachel's mom went away.
"I hug whoever I want!" Tammy declared.

"No, we don't hug everyone," I explained. "We only
hug people we really know and love, like a good
friend or a close family member."

"You know, Mom," Guy mumbled, "I really don't like being hugged."
"If you don't like being hugged, you can just say: 'I don't like that,'" I said.
Guy looked at me and nodded.

We continued along our way, two small hands
in two big hands, a mom and her kids.

We stopped by our favorite ice
cream shop for a treat.
"Hello, I'd like two cones, please.
One strawberry, one vanilla."
"See, Tammy?" Guy whispered,
"Mommy's not hugging the
ice cream man because
he's not her friend!"

After we got the cones, I explained to the kids:
"It's the ice cream man's job to serve us ice cream, so I say hi to him politely
and make my order. If we see people but we don't really know them, we
usually just say hi to them."

"Wait... What about Mr. Pete from kindergarten? We see him every morning and we know him," Tammy said.

"Yes, you know Mr. Pete, but he's not your friend. His job is to take care of the school, so when we meet him, we don't hug and kiss. We just say good morning," I answered.

"He always shakes my hand and calls me Mr. President!" Guy said, giggling.

"He gives me three high fives," Tammy added.

"Mr. Pete is a very nice custodian. You can greet him with handshakes and high fives."

We left the ice cream shop and walked home, two small hands in two big ones, a mom and her kids.

On the way, we met a couple of people we knew from town: our
new neighbor, Ethan, and our friend Nathan's big sister, Sally.

When we reached the playground, Guy and Tammy asked if they
could play for a while, so I sat on a bench and watched them.
Guy pushed Tammy on the swings. Then a woman
went over to them and held out some candy.

As I rushed over to them, I heard Tammy say, "We don't know you. You're a stranger. Mommy and Daddy told us not to take things from strangers."
Tammy and Guy ran over to me and hugged me tight.

"I'm sorry," the woman said. "I didn't mean to frighten your children. I just wanted to give them some candy. I should have asked you first." Then she went to play with her own kids.

"Well done, Tammy!" I said. "I'm proud of you for not taking the candy."
"I wanted to take it," Guy said. "I love candy! And that woman was nice!"

"I know you love candy, but do you know that woman?" I asked.
"No... " they answered. "Even if that lady seemed nice, she's still a stranger.
Remember what Daddy and I always say?"

"Never take candy from strangers," Tammy said.

"Never take anything from strangers," Guy said.

"And never go anywhere with strangers, no matter what they say," they chimed in together.

"Right!" I said. "Even if a stranger says they need your help, you never go without Mom and Dad."

"Ms. Violet always tells us that kids should only help kids and adults help adults," Guy added.

"That's right! Kids don't need to help adults. Adults will find a way to manage on their own."

THANK YOU!

"But what if we need help?" Tammy asked.

"If you need help, and there's no one around that you know, try to find parents with kids. Ask them to call me or Daddy. You know our phone numbers and our address by heart."

"Mom, remember when I got lost at the amusement park and I cried a lot?" Guy asked.
"Of course I do! I was very worried about you. But you did the right thing.
You asked a lady with kids to call me."

"And they waited with me until you came to get me," smiled Guy.
"Right. You didn't go anywhere with her," I pointed out.

"But what if it's someone that I know, like Rachel's mom? I can go with her, right?"
"Only if me or Daddy say you can. Never go anywhere without our permission."
"But yesterday, Grandma and Grandpa picked us up from kindergarten," Guy reminded me.

"What do you two think? Is it okay to go with Grandma and Grandpa?"
Guy and Tammy looked at each other. They weren't sure what to say.

"Of course, it's okay," I explained. "Grandma and Grandpa are part of our close family. Plus, that morning I told you and Ms. Violet that they would be picking you up, right? I would never send someone to pick you up without telling you and Ms. Violet."

"I love it when Grandma and Grandpa pick us up from kindergarten and take us out!" Guy exclaimed. We all smiled.

We got home before dark, a mom with her kids, two small hands in two big hands.

While Dad made dinner, the doorbell rang. Guy ran to open the door.
It was the postman with a package.
"See that, Daddy? I opened the door all by myself. I'm a big boy!"
Guy said proudly.

"You opened the door to a stranger! You didn't even ask who it was!" Tammy shouted.
"Tammy's right," said Daddy. "When you hear the doorbell ring, you ask, 'Who is it?',
but you don't open the door. You call me or Mommy."

Guy frowned quietly.

"Is the postman someone we know?" Daddy asked.

"No, he's a stranger. But what if he says he's
a postman and that he has Mommy's mail?"
Guy asked, confused.

"You can never really know who's behind the door. Without our permission, you should never open the door to anyone, no matter what they say."

"I think I can tell if a person is bad and I'll know to be careful," Tammy said. "A bad person wears dark clothes and has a scary face."

"No, Tammy. You're wrong. Bad people can seem very friendly. They can wear nice clothes. It's hard to tell who's bad and who's good. That's why we need to learn to be careful."

After their bath, the kids got into their beds and Daddy sat down between them.
"Daddy, today we met all kinds of people..." Guy told him.

"Some we knew, some were strangers,"
Tammy added.
"But all of them were nice," Guy said.

"Sounds like you had an interesting day," Daddy said.
"It was also kind of scary..." Tammy said.

"Why scary?" asked Daddy.
"Because there are bad people, too, and we can't know who they are. That's scary for me," Tammy said, reaching over to hold Daddy's hand.

"Most people in the world are good, but there are some bad people too,"
Daddy explained, stroking Tammy's hair.
"Those are the people we have to watch out for," Guy said.

"What do I always say, kids?" Daddy asked with a smile.
"You and Mommy trust that we know how to keep ourselves safe,"
Guy and Tammy said together.
"And of course, we're always here for you to answer any questions and help
you solve any problems," I added. "We'll never be angry about what you tell us."

"Can I have a hug?" asked Tammy.
"And I want a goodnight kiss," said Guy.
Daddy and I hugged and kissed our
precious children, Tammy and Guy, and
we all curled up together.

Yael Feder
The Safety Book
Strangers and Dangers

With love and appreciation for the actresses of my theater,
who spend each day teaching boys and girls to look out
for themselves.

1   2   3   4   5   6   7   8   9   10

This publication or any part thereof may not be reproduced,
photographed, recorded, broadcasted, translated, scanned,
stored in a database, or distributed in any form or by any
electronic or mechanical means, including the internet,
electronic book, computer, tablet, cellphone or other media
format, without the written permission of the publisher.

Copyright by Schocken Publishing House Ltd., Tel Aviv
www.schocken.co.il
Typeset and Design: Schocken Publishing House, 2022
ISBN 978-965-19-1141-5

Printed in Great Britain
by Amazon

43819452R10016